Pebble® Plus

Patterns in Nature

Seasons of the Year

by Margaret Hall

Consulting Editor: Gail Saunders-Smith, PhD

Content Consultant: Dr. Ronald Browne, Associate Professor of Elementary Education
Minnesota State University, Mankato, Minnesota

Capstone press®

Mankato, Minnesota

Pebble Plus is published by Capstone Press,
151 Good Counsel Drive, P.O. Box 669, Mankato, Minnesota 56002.
www.capstonepress.com

1 2 3 4 5 6 11 10 09 08 07 06

Library of Congress Cataloging-in-Publication Data
Hall, Margaret, 1947–
    Seasons of the year / by Margaret Hall.
    p. cm.— (Pebble plus. Patterns in nature)
    Includes bibliographical references and index.
    ISBN-13: 978-0-7368-6341-4 (hardcover)
    ISBN-10: 0-7368-6341-9 (hardcover)
    ISBN-13: 978-0-7368-9618-4 (softcover pbk.)
    ISBN-10: 0-7368-9618-X (softcover pbk.)
    1. Seasons—Juvenile literature. 2. Pattern perception—Juvenile literature. I. Title. II. Series.
QB637.4.H35 2007
508.2—dc22
          2006001456

Summary: Simple text and photographs present an introduction to why the seasons change and how seasons
are a recurring pattern in nature.

Editorial Credits
Heather Adamson, editor; Kia Adams, designer; Renée Doyle, illustrator; Jo Miller, photo researcher
    Scott Thoms, photo editor

Photo Credits
Corbis/Ariel Skelley, 5; Roy Morsch, 13
Peter Arnold/Clyde H. Smith, 1; Peter Frischmuth, 10–11
PhotoEdit, Inc./Dennis MacDonald, 21 (all)
Shutterstock/Andres Rodriguez, cover (sunflowers); Kevin Britland, 9 (right); Konstantin Povod, 15;
    Paul-Andre Belle-Isle, cover (winter scene); Ron Hilton, 9 (left); Telnova Olya, back cover; Weldon
    Schlonegar, cover (autumn highway); WizData, cover (buds), 16–17

Note to Parents and Teachers

The Patterns in Nature set supports national science standards related to earth
and life science. This book describes and illustrates the seasons of the year.
The images support early readers in understanding the text. The repetition of words and
phrases helps early readers learn new words. This book also introduces early readers
to subject-specific vocabulary words, which are defined in the Glossary section. Early
readers may need assistance to read some words and to use the Table of Contents,
Glossary, Read More, Internet Sites, and Index sections of the book.

Table of Contents

What Makes the Seasons?

Summer, autumn, winter,
and spring.
Daylight makes the seasons
of the year.

Light and heat hit the Earth

as it orbits the sun.

The Earth is tilted.

The amount of daylight

changes during the year

because of the tilt.

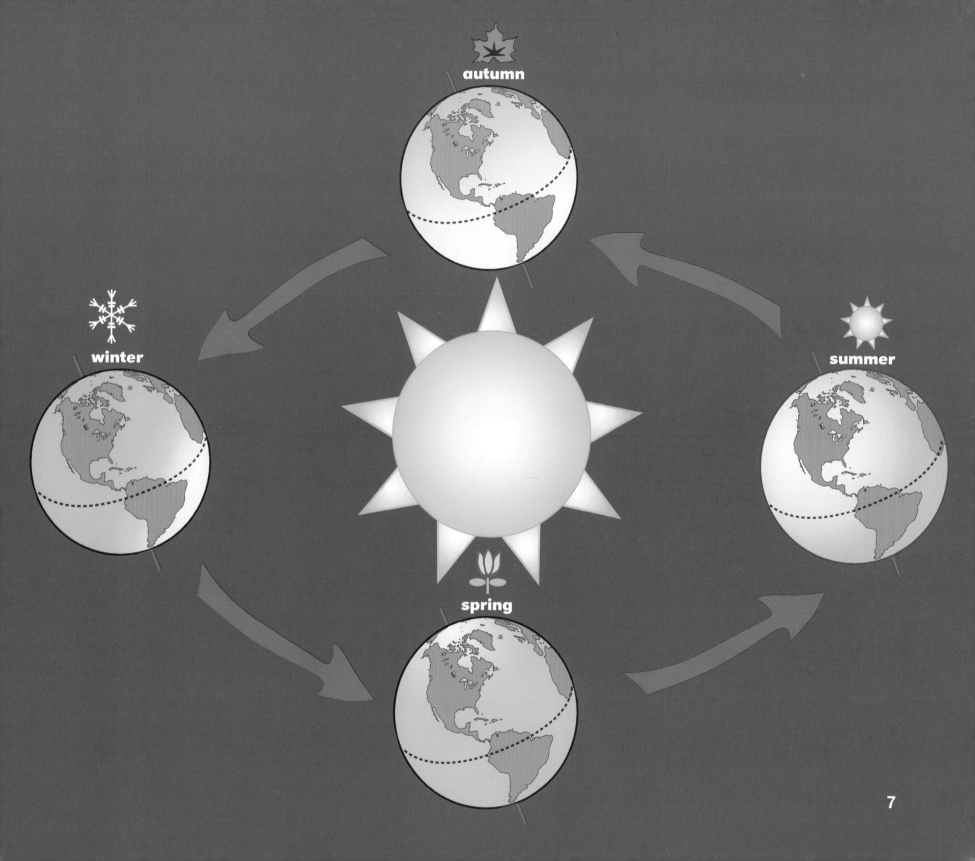

autumn

winter

summer

spring

7

The sun's light and warmth

change Earth's seasons.

Each season has

different weather.

Seasons last about three months.

The Seasons

Summer has lots of daylight.

The weather is warm.

Your part of Earth tilts

toward the sun in summer.

Warm summer cools

into autumn.

Leaves turn colors and fall

from the trees.

Animals get ready for winter.

Daylight hours are short

in winter.

The weather is cold or snowy.

Your part of Earth tilts away

from the sun in winter.

In spring, daylight hours
get longer again.
Leaves and plants
start to grow.
It can be very rainy.

Seasons aren't the same
everywhere at the same time.
It's summer in the north
when it's winter in the south.

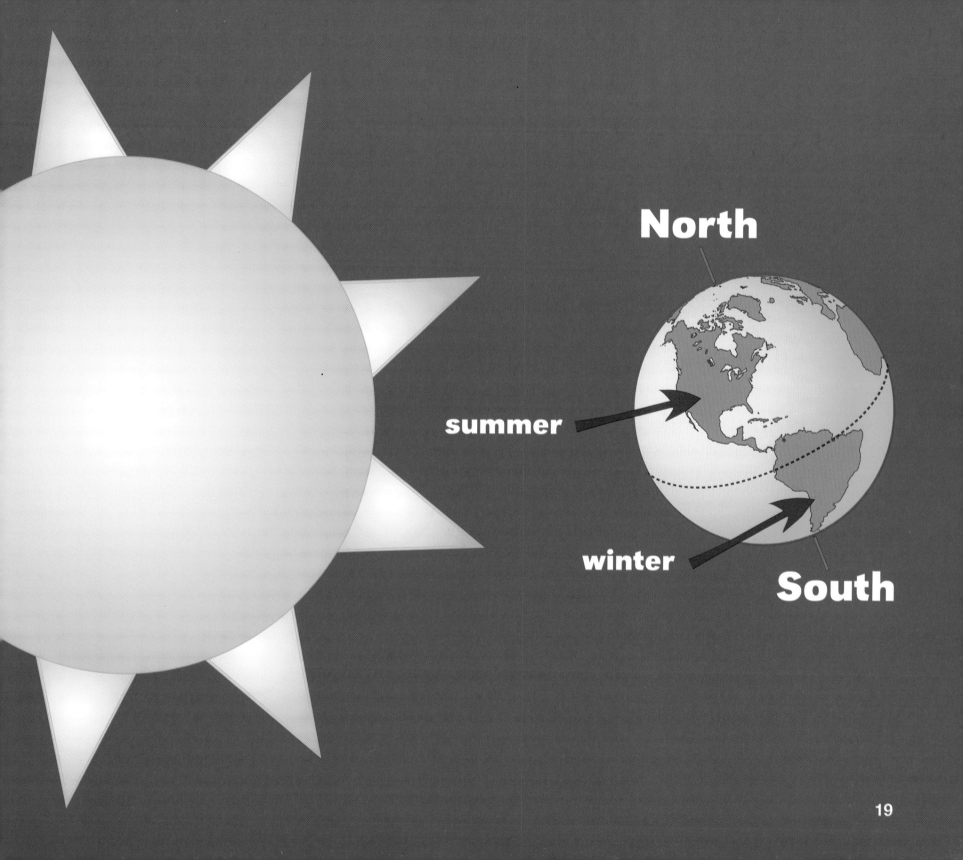

North

summer

winter

South

It's a Pattern

Earth always orbits the sun.

Seasons keep changing

in the same pattern.

Summer will come again.

Then autumn, winter,

and spring.

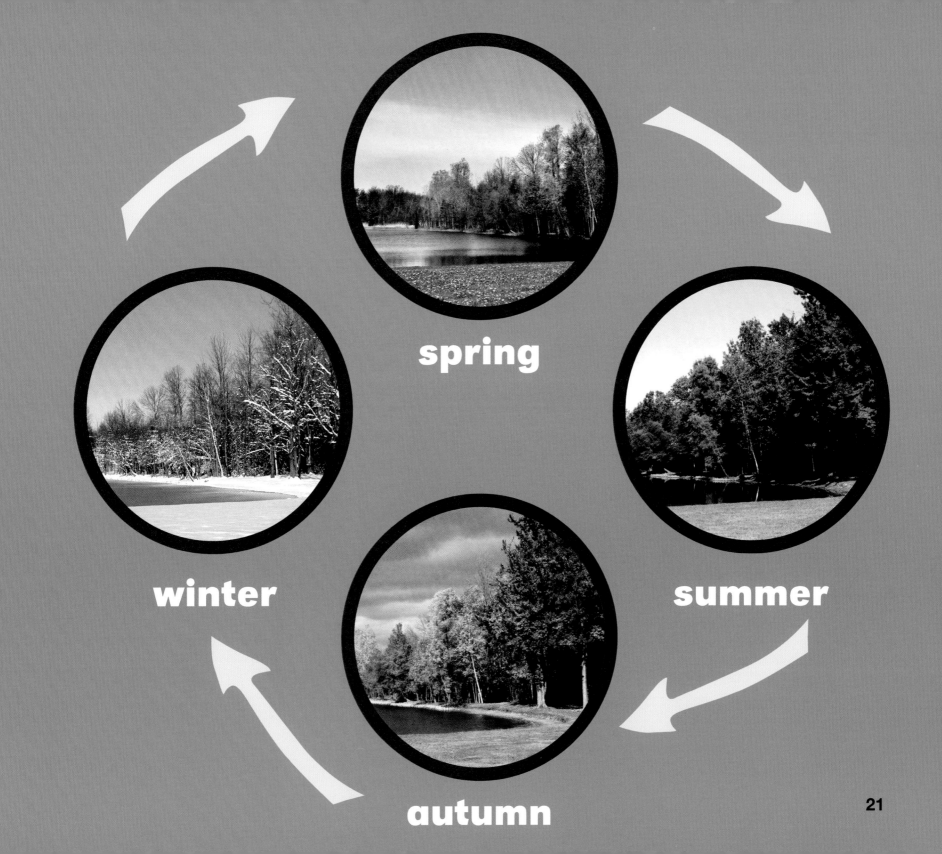

spring

summer

autumn

winter

Glossary

autumn—the season when days start to get shorter and cooler

orbit—to travel around an object in space, such as the sun or a planet

pattern—something that happens again and again in the same order

season—a time of the year; most seasons in North America last about 3 months.

spring—the season when days start to get longer and warmer

summer—the season when days are long and hot

tilt—an angle or lean; not straight

winter—the season when days are short and cold

Read More

Birch, Robin. *Earth, Sun, and Moon.* Space Series. Philadelphia: Chelsea Clubhouse, 2003.

DeGezelle, Terri. *Summer.* Seasons. Mankato, Minn.: Capstone Press, 2003.

Whitehouse, Patricia. *Seasons 123.* Seasons. Chicago: Heinemann, 2003.

Internet Sites

FactHound offers a safe, fun way to find Internet sites related to this book. All of the sites on FactHound have been researched by our staff.

Here's how:

1. Go to *www.facthound.com*

2. Choose your grade level.

3. Type in this book ID **0736863419** for age-appropriate sites. You may also browse subjects by clicking on letters, or by clicking on pictures and words.

4. Click on the **Fetch It** button.

FactHound will fetch the best sites for you!

Index

Word Count: 176
Grade: 1
Early-Intervention Level: 16